HOW TO RAISE GOATS

A Beginners Guide to Building and Running a Successful
Goat Farming Enterprise

MORRIS WILLIS

TABLE OF CONTENTS

INTRODUCTION

Goats are a versatile and captivating species that have been intertwined with human civilization for millennia. Whether you envision them as a source of wholesome milk, succulent meat, luxurious wool, or simply as endearing companions, goats have proven themselves to be valuable additions to farms and homesteads. In this comprehensive guide, we delve into the intricate world of goat rearing, offering a wealth of knowledge and practical advice to beginners and enthusiasts alike.

"The Complete Guide to Raising Happy and Healthy Goats" is your key to unlocking the secrets of successful goat husbandry. Within these pages, we will traverse the vast terrain of goat farming, from understanding the diverse breeds that grace our farms to mastering the intricacies of their care, health, and management. Whether you are a novice yearning for the enchantment of a backyard goat or an experienced hand yearning to enhance your expertise, this guide will be your steadfast companion, offering insights, strategies, and wisdom garnered from generations of dedicated goat enthusiasts.

Goats, those enigmatic and charming creatures, have been woven into the fabric of human existence for countless generations. They have traversed landscapes and cultures, offering sustenance, companionship, and livelihoods to those who have embraced their presence. Yet, to venture into goat farming is to embark on a partnership that demands understanding, responsibility, and compassion. As with any journey, preparation and knowledge lay the foundation for a rewarding and harmonious experience.

This guide will lead you through the nuanced world of goat husbandry, from selecting the perfect breed to nurturing kids and understanding the art of milking. We will delve into the realms of nutrition, health care, and breeding, equipping you with the tools to ensure the wellbeing of your caprine companions. You will discover the gratification of transforming goat fibers into exquisite textiles and explore the delicate balance of goat behavior and training.

Moreover, we shall explore the broader dimensions of sustainable and organic goat farming, touching upon the importance of ethical practices and environmentally conscious choices. Whether you dream of indulging in the delights of goat cheese, adorning your life with luxurious fiber products, or simply basking in the joy of goat company, this guide will accompany you on your journey.

So, whether you are contemplating the addition of a few goats to your family homestead or envisioning a thriving goat enterprise, embark with us on a voyage of discovery. Let us unravel the mysteries of goat farming, navigate the challenges, and celebrate the triumphs together. Welcome to "The Complete Guide to Raising Happy and Healthy Goats," your gateway to a fulfilling and enriching connection with these remarkable animals.

Chapter 1:
Goat Farming

Goat farming, once a staple of pastoral and rural life, has now emerged as a fascinating and promising venture for modern farmers and enthusiasts alike. With a history dating back thousands of years, goats have played an essential role in providing milk, meat, and fiber to diverse cultures around the world. Today, the appeal of raising goats extends beyond tradition, capturing the attention of individuals seeking sustainable agriculture, wholesome nutrition, and even charming animal companions. This introduction to goat farming will explore the allure of raising goats, the characteristics of different goat breeds, and how to set goals that align with your aspirations.

The Appeal of Raising Goats:

1. Sustainability and Self Sufficiency:
Goats are renowned for their remarkable ability to thrive in a variety of environments, making them a suitable choice for farmers who value sustainable and self sufficient practices. Their adaptability allows them to graze on a wide range of vegetation, reducing the need for expensive feed and minimizing environmental impact.

2. Nutrient Rich Products:
Whether you're interested in goat milk, meat, or fiber, you'll be rewarded with nutrient rich products that contribute to a wholesome diet. Goat milk, for instance, is not only packed with

essential vitamins and minerals but is also easier to digest for those who are lactose intolerant.

3. Fiber Arts and Crafts:
Certain goat breeds, such as Angora and Cashmere goats, offer luxurious and sought after fibers that can be transformed into exquisite textiles. These fibers are prized by artisans and crafters for their softness and ability to create garments and accessories of exceptional quality.

4. Natural Land Management:
Goats' natural foraging behavior can be harnessed for land management purposes. They can help control invasive plants and weeds, reducing the need for chemical interventions on your property.

5. Animal Companionship:
Beyond their practical benefits, goats have an endearing and charming quality that makes them excellent animal companions. Many goat owners find joy in the companionship and unique personalities of their goats.

Different Goat Breeds and Their Characteristics:

Goats come in a variety of breeds, each with its distinct characteristics and attributes. When choosing a breed, consider your specific goals and the environment in which you intend to raise them. Here are a few popular goat breeds and their notable features:

1. Nubian:
Known for their distinctive long ears and gentle disposition, Nubian goats are prized for their high milk production and rich, creamy milk. They thrive in diverse climates and are well suited for both milk and meat production.

2. Boer:
Boer goats are renowned for their robust meat production qualities. They are hardy, fast growing, and have a remarkable ability to thrive in challenging conditions.

3. Angora:
Angora goats are treasured for their luxurious mohair fiber, which is used to create high quality textiles and garments. They require regular shearing and meticulous care.

4. Saanen:
Saanen goats are excellent milk producers, known for their mild temperament and high milk yield. They are popular in dairy operations and contribute to various dairy products.

5. Cashmere:
Cashmere goats produce the highly sought after cashmere fiber, renowned for its softness and warmth. Raising cashmere goats requires attention to their specialized needs for fiber production.

Setting Your Goals: Milk, Meat, Fiber, or Pets:

Before embarking on your goat farming journey, it's essential to define your goals and aspirations. The purpose for which you raise goats will influence your choice of breed, management practices, and overall approach to farming. Consider the following goals:

1. Milk Production:
If your primary goal is milk production, breeds like Nubian, Saanen, and Alpine goats are excellent choices. They are known for their high milk yields and the quality of milk they produce.

2. Meat Production:
For meat production, breeds like Boer and Kiko goats are favored due to their robust build, fast growth, and efficient meat conversion.

3. Fiber Production:
If you're interested in fiber arts and crafts, breeds like Angora and Cashmere goats offer luxurious fibers that can be transformed into textiles and garments.

4. Pets and Companions:
Goats also make wonderful pets and companions. Their playful and curious nature can bring joy and enrichment to your life, even if you're not focused on specific agricultural outputs.

In conclusion, goat farming offers a diverse range of opportunities, from providing nutrient rich products to contributing to sustainable land management. The appeal of raising goats extends beyond practical benefits, encompassing a deep connection to agricultural heritage and a fulfilling way of life. Whether you're drawn to the idea of producing wholesome food, crafting exquisite textiles, or simply enjoying the company of these charming animals, goat farming has something to offer for everyone. As you delve deeper into the world of goat farming, you'll discover the unique rewards and challenges that come with each breed and endeavor.

Chapter 2:
Selecting the Right Goats

Selecting the right goats for your farm is a critical decision that can significantly impact the success and sustainability of your goat farming venture. Whether you're interested in milk production, meat, fiber, or simply companionship, making informed choices during the selection process is essential. This guide will walk you through the process of evaluating different goat breeds based on your purpose, ensuring the health and quality of the animals you choose, and buying goats from reputable sources to set the stage for a successful and fulfilling goat farming experience.

Evaluating Breeds for Your Purpose:

The first step in selecting the right goats is to determine your specific goals and purposes for raising them. Each goat breed has unique characteristics that make it well suited for certain tasks. Understanding these characteristics will help you choose the breed that aligns with your objectives. Here's a closer look at some common purposes and the breeds that excel in each area:

1. Milk Production:
If your primary goal is milk production, consider breeds like:

- Nubian: Known for high butterfat content and excellent milk yield.
- Saanen: Renowned for their consistent milk production and gentle temperament.

- Alpine: A versatile breed with good milk production and adaptability to various climates.

2. Meat Production:

For meat production, look into breeds such as:

- Boer: Prized for their rapid growth, efficient meat conversion, and robust build.
- Kiko: Known for their hardiness, parasite resistance, and meat quality.
- Spanish: Favored for their adaptability and lean meat production.

3. Fiber Production:

If you're interested in fiber production, consider:

- Angora: Sought after for their luxurious mohair fiber, which is used in textiles and crafts.
- Cashmere: Valued for their fine cashmere fiber, which is prized for its softness and warmth.

4. Companionship and Pets:

For companionship or pets, friendly and docile breeds like:

- Pygmy: Miniature goats with playful personalities, making them delightful companions.
- Nigerian Dwarf: Small, colorful goats known for their friendly nature and adaptability.

Choosing Healthy and Quality Animals:

Once you've determined the breed that suits your purpose, it's crucial to select healthy and high quality animals to form the foundation of your herd. Healthy goats not only ensure the success of your farming venture but also minimize the risk of disease transmission. Here are important factors to consider when evaluating the health and quality of goats:

1. Physical Appearance:

Observe the goats' overall appearance. They should have clear, bright eyes; clean ears and nostrils; and a well groomed coat. Check for any signs of lameness or difficulty in movement.

2. Body Condition:

Assess the body condition of the goats. They should have a healthy weight, neither too thin nor too obese. A healthy body condition is indicative of proper nutrition and care.

3. Coat and Skin:

Inspect the goats' coats for signs of parasites, such as lice or mites. Healthy goats should have smooth, glossy coats and healthy skin.

4. Hooves:

Check the condition of the hooves. Overgrown or cracked hooves can lead to discomfort and health issues.

5. Behavior:

Observe the goats' behavior. They should be alert, curious, and responsive. Avoid goats that appear lethargic or overly aggressive.

6. Documentation:
Request relevant documentation from the seller, including health records, vaccination history, and any registration papers for registered breeds.

Buying Goats from Reputable Sources:

Purchasing goats from reputable and trustworthy sources is essential to ensure that you're acquiring healthy and well cared for animals. Here's how to identify reputable sources and make a wise purchasing decision:

1. Certified Breeders:
Consider buying goats from certified breeders who are knowledgeable about the breed's characteristics, health requirements, and proper care. Certified breeders are more likely to provide accurate information and offer support.

2. Local Farms and Breeders:
Supporting local farms and breeders can be beneficial as you can visit the farm, see the living conditions of the goats, and ask questions about their care and management.

3. Avoid Online Auctions:
While online platforms may offer convenience, it's advisable to avoid purchasing goats from online auctions where you can't physically assess the animals' health and condition.

4. References and Reviews:

Seek references and read reviews from other buyers who have purchased goats from the same source. Positive reviews and recommendations are indicators of a reputable seller.

5. Quarantine:

Upon bringing new goats to your farm, it's essential to quarantine them for a period of time before introducing them to your existing herd. This practice helps prevent the potential spread of diseases.

6. Veterinarian Inspection:

Consider having a veterinarian inspect the goats before finalizing the purchase. A veterinarian can provide a thorough health assessment and ensure that the goats are free from any contagious diseases.

Selecting the right goats for your farm involves a thoughtful and informed process that takes into account your goals, breed characteristics, and the health and quality of the animals. By evaluating breeds based on your purpose, ensuring the health of the goats you choose, and buying from reputable sources, you're laying a strong foundation for a successful and rewarding goat farming venture. Remember that each goat you bring into your farm contributes not only to your agricultural goals but also to the legacy of responsible and compassionate animal husbandry.

Chapter 3:
Creating the Ideal Goat Habitat

Creating a suitable and comfortable habitat for your goats is essential for their wellbeing, health, and productivity. A well designed goat habitat ensures that your animals have proper shelter, access to nutritious food and clean water, and a safe environment to thrive in. In this chapter, we will explore the key components of an ideal goat habitat, including designing shelter and housing, effective fencing and pasture management, and providing clean water and proper nutrition. By implementing these essential elements, you can create a habitat that promotes the health and happiness of your goats while optimizing your goat farming operation.

Designing Shelter and Housing

Adequate shelter is crucial to protect your goats from harsh weather conditions, provide a comfortable resting place, and minimize stress. When designing shelter and housing for your goats, consider the following factors:

1. Size and Space:
Ensure that the shelter is spacious enough to accommodate all your goats comfortably. The general rule of thumb is to provide at least 1520 square feet per adult goat. This space allows them to move around, rest, and engage in natural behaviors.

2. Ventilation:

Good ventilation is essential to prevent the buildup of moisture, odors, and harmful gases inside the shelter. Proper airflow helps maintain a healthy environment and reduces the risk of respiratory issues.

3. Orientation:
Position the shelter to provide protection from prevailing winds and direct sunlight. A south facing orientation can help capture sunlight during colder months, providing natural warmth.

4. Bedding:
Use clean and dry bedding material, such as straw or wood shavings, to create a comfortable resting area for your goats. Regularly clean and replace bedding to maintain hygiene.

5. Separate Areas:
Design separate areas for feeding, resting, and kidding (birthing). This segregation helps prevent feed contamination, stress, and provides a safe space for newborns.

Fencing and Pasture Management

Effective fencing and pasture management are crucial for providing your goats with space to roam, graze, and engage in natural behaviors. Proper fencing also helps keep predators out and minimizes the risk of goats escaping. Consider the following aspects when planning your fencing and pasture management:

1. Fencing Materials:

Choose sturdy and goatproof fencing materials, such as woven wire, electric fencing, or welded wire. Ensure that the fencing is tall enough to prevent goats from jumping or climbing over.

2. Grazing Area:

Designate a grazing area that provides enough space for your goats to forage and graze. Rotate grazing areas to prevent overgrazing and promote healthy pasture growth.

3. Shade and Shelter:

Ensure that your pasture has natural or built-in shade to protect goats from excessive sunlight. Shade structures can help prevent heat stress during hot weather.

4. Pasture Management:

Practice rotational grazing to prevent pasture depletion and encourage regrowth. Regularly monitor the condition of the pasture and adjust the rotation schedule as needed.

5. Forage Diversity:

Offer a variety of forage options, including grasses, legumes, and browse, to provide a balanced diet and encourage natural browsing behavior.

Providing Clean Water and Proper Nutrition

Access to clean water and a balanced diet are fundamental to the health and productivity of your goats. Proper nutrition supports growth, milk production, and overall wellbeing. Consider the following guidelines for providing clean water and nutrition:

1. Clean Water Supply:
Ensure a constant supply of clean, fresh water for your goats. Use clean water troughs that are elevated to prevent contamination and kept at a suitable height for easy access.

2. Nutritional Requirements:
Understand the nutritional requirements of your goats based on their age, purpose (milk, meat, fiber), and reproductive status. Consult a veterinarian or livestock nutritionist to develop a balanced feeding program.

3. Feed Storage:
Store feed in a dry and secure area to prevent spoilage and contamination. Use proper containers and follow recommended storage practices.

4. Supplements:
Provide necessary mineral supplements to address any nutritional deficiencies in your goats' diet. Consult with a veterinarian to determine the appropriate mineral supplementation.

5. Feeding Schedule:
Establish a consistent feeding schedule to ensure that your goats receive their required nutrients at regular intervals. Avoid sudden changes in diet, as it can lead to digestive issues.

6. Monitoring and Adjustments:

Regularly monitor the body condition of your goats and adjust their diet as needed. Overfeeding or underfeeding can lead to health problems and decreased productivity.

Creating the ideal goat habitat involves careful planning and attention to detail. By designing suitable shelter and housing, implementing effective fencing and pasture management strategies, and providing clean water and proper nutrition, you can ensure the health, comfort, and productivity of your goats. A well-designed habitat not only contributes to the wellbeing of your animals but also enhances the overall success of your goat farming venture. As you prioritize the needs of your goats and create a nurturing environment, you'll witness the positive impact on their growth, behavior, and quality of life.

Chapter 4:
Goat Nutrition and Feeding

Providing proper nutrition is a cornerstone of successful goat farming. A well-balanced diet ensures the overall health, growth, reproduction, and productivity of your goats. In this chapter, we will delve into the essential aspects of goat nutrition and feeding. We will explore understanding the basic nutritional needs of goats, choosing and preparing feeds, and implementing strategies to prevent overeating and nutritional disorders. By mastering the art of goat nutrition and feeding, you can optimize the wellbeing and performance of your goats, leading to a thriving and sustainable goat farming operation.

Understanding Basic Nutritional Needs:

Goats, like all livestock, have specific nutritional requirements that must be met to maintain their health and vitality. To ensure that your goats receive the proper nutrients, it's essential to understand their basic nutritional needs and the role of different nutrients in their diet:

1. Energy:
Energy is a vital component of a goat's diet and is necessary for growth, maintenance, and production. Carbohydrates, such as grains and forages, are the primary source of energy for goats.

2. Protein:
Protein is essential for muscle development, milk production, and overall body functions. Good sources of protein include legumes,

such as alfalfa and clover, as well as soybean meal and other protein supplements.

3. Vitamins:

Vitamins play a crucial role in various metabolic processes and overall health. Goats require vitamins A, D, and E, among others. Vitamin deficiencies can lead to health issues and reduced productivity.

4. Minerals:

Minerals are essential for bone health, enzyme function, and various physiological processes. Common minerals needed by goats include calcium, phosphorus, selenium, and zinc.

5. Water:

Water is perhaps the most critical nutrient. Access to clean and fresh water at all times is essential for digestion, temperature regulation, and overall wellbeing.

Choosing and Preparing Feeds:

Choosing the right feeds and preparing balanced rations are key factors in meeting your goats' nutritional needs. Here's how to make informed choices and prepare feeds effectively:

1. Forages:

Forages, such as hay and pasture, should form the bulk of a goat's diet. Select high-quality forages that are free from mold, dust, and contaminants. Rotate pastures to prevent overgrazing and ensure a variety of nutrients.

2. Grains and Concentrates:

Grains and concentrates can supplement forages to provide additional energy and protein. Common grains include corn, oats, and barley. When offering grains, start with small amounts and gradually increase to prevent digestive upset.

3. Protein Supplements:

If your goats' forage lacks sufficient protein, consider offering protein supplements like soybean meal, alfalfa pellets, or other commercially available protein sources.

4. Mineral Supplements:

Provide a mineral supplement formulated specifically for goats. Mineral deficiencies can lead to health issues, so ensure that your goats have access to a balanced mineral mix at all times.

5. Avoid Overfeeding:

Overfeeding can lead to obesity and related health problems. Calculate your goats' nutritional needs based on their weight, age, and purpose to avoid excessive consumption.

6. Feed Presentation:

Present feeds in clean and appropriate containers to prevent contamination and waste. Elevated feeders can help keep feeds clean and reduce the risk of parasite transmission.

Preventing Overeating and Nutritional Disorders:

Maintaining proper feeding practices is crucial to prevent overeating and the development of nutritional disorders. Here are strategies to ensure your goats receive the right amount of nutrients without overindulging:

1. Feeding Schedule:

Establish a consistent feeding schedule to regulate your goats' intake. Offering feeds at the same times each day helps prevent binge eating and digestive issues.

2. Monitor Body Condition:

Regularly assess the body condition of your goats to ensure they are neither underweight nor overweight. Adjust their diet as needed to maintain a healthy body condition score.

3. Avoid Rapid Diet Changes:

Goats have sensitive digestive systems, so avoid sudden changes in their diet. Gradually introduce new feeds or make adjustments to prevent digestive upset.

4. Limit Treats and Supplements:

While treats and supplements can be enjoyable for goats, they should be given in moderation. Excessive treats can lead to imbalanced nutrition and obesity.

5. Provide Adequate Roughage:

Adequate roughage, such as hay and pasture, helps prevent overeating by promoting satiety. Goats should have access to roughage at all times.

6. Monitor Weight Gain:

Regularly weigh your goats to track their weight gain and growth. Sudden or excessive weight gain may indicate overeating or an imbalanced diet.

Goat nutrition and feeding are fundamental aspects of successful goat farming. By understanding the basic nutritional needs of your goats, choosing and preparing appropriate feeds, and implementing strategies to prevent overeating and nutritional disorders, you can ensure the health, productivity, and overall wellbeing of your animals. Proper nutrition contributes to optimal growth, milk production, and reproductive success, while also reducing the risk of health issues. As you prioritize the nutritional needs of your goats and create a well-balanced feeding regimen, you'll witness the positive impact on their vitality, performance, and overall quality of life.

Chapter 5:
Health and Veterinary Care

Maintaining the health and wellbeing of your goats is paramount to the success of your goat farming venture. A robust health management plan, combined with timely identification and treatment of common goat ailments, ensures that your goats thrive and remain productive. In this chapter, we will explore the essential aspects of goat health and veterinary care. We will discuss the development of a health management plan, methods for identifying and treating common goat ailments, and guidelines for working with veterinarians and administering medications. By prioritizing goat health, you can establish a foundation of wellness that contributes to the long-term success of your goat farming operation.

Developing a Health Management Plan

A comprehensive health management plan is a proactive approach to maintaining the health of your goats. It involves preventive measures, regular monitoring, and prompt response to any health issues. Here's how to develop an effective health management plan:

1. Biosecurity Measures:
Implement biosecurity practices to prevent the introduction and spread of diseases. Quarantine new goats before introducing them to the herd and restrict access to your farm to minimize disease transmission.

2. Vaccination Schedule:
Consult with a veterinarian to establish a vaccination schedule that aligns with your region's prevalent diseases. Common vaccinations may include protection against diseases like tetanus, enterotoxemia, and respiratory infections.

3. Parasite Management:
Develop a deworming schedule to control internal and external parasites. Rotate dewormers and avoid overusing them to prevent parasite resistance.

4. Nutrition and Feeding:
Provide a balanced and nutritious diet to support your goats' immune system and overall health. Ensure access to clean water, high-quality forages, and appropriate supplements.

5. Housing and Environment:
Maintain a clean and well-ventilated living environment for your goats. Regularly clean bedding, remove waste, and ensure proper drainage to prevent the buildup of moisture and pathogens.

6. Observation and Record Keeping:
Regularly observe your goats for any signs of illness, changes in behavior, or abnormalities. Keep detailed records of healthrelated information, including vaccinations, treatments, and observations.

Identifying and Treating Common Goat Ailments

Despite preventive measures, goats can still experience health issues. Timely identification and proper treatment are crucial to minimizing the impact of these ailments. Here are some common goat ailments and steps for identification and treatment:

1. Internal Parasites:
Symptoms: Weight loss, lethargy, poor coat condition, and diarrhea.
Treatment: Administer appropriate dewormers as directed by a veterinarian. Rotate dewormers to prevent resistance.

2. Respiratory Infections:
Symptoms: Coughing, nasal discharge, rapid breathing, and lethargy.
Treatment: Provide supportive care, such as a clean and dry environment, along with prescribed antibiotics from a veterinarian.

3. Foot Rot:
Symptoms: Lameness, swelling, foul odor, and discharge around the hooves.
Treatment: Isolate affected goats, trim overgrown hooves, and provide treatment as prescribed by a veterinarian.

4. Scours (Diarrhea):
Symptoms: Watery or bloody diarrhea, dehydration, lethargy, and decreased appetite.

Treatment: Address the underlying cause, provide electrolytes to combat dehydration, and administer probiotics under veterinary guidance.

5. Coccidiosis:
Symptoms: Diarrhea, lethargy, dehydration, and weight loss.
Treatment: Administer appropriate coccidiostats as recommended by a veterinarian. Maintain a clean and dry environment.

6. Pregnancy related Issues:
Symptoms: Difficulty kidding, retained placenta, and pregnancy toxemia.
Treatment: Provide assistance during kidding if necessary, address retained placenta promptly, and manage nutritional needs during late pregnancy to prevent pregnancy toxemia.

Working with Veterinarians and Administering Medications

Collaboration with a veterinarian is essential for maintaining goat health. A veterinarian can provide guidance, diagnose illnesses, and recommend appropriate treatments. Here's how to work effectively with veterinarians and administer medications:

1. Establish a Veterinary Relationship:
Connect with a veterinarian who has experience in goat health. Schedule regular checkups and maintain open communication for prompt intervention when needed.

2. Diagnostic Testing:

When a goat exhibits unusual symptoms, consult your veterinarian for diagnostic testing. Tests such as bloodwork, fecal exams, and cultures can help identify the underlying issue.

3. Administering Medications:
Follow your veterinarian's instructions precisely when administering medications. Administer oral medications, injections, and other treatments as directed to ensure proper dosage and effectiveness.

4. Withdrawal Periods:
Be aware of withdrawal periods for medications used in food-producing animals. Adhere to these periods to ensure that meat and milk remain safe for consumption.

5. Record Keeping:
Maintain accurate records of veterinary visits, treatments, medications, and outcomes. These records assist in tracking health trends and making informed decisions.

6. Emergency Preparedness:
Develop an emergency plan in consultation with your veterinarian. Be prepared to address sudden health crises and have necessary medications and supplies on hand.

A focus on goat health and veterinary care is central to successful goat farming. By developing a comprehensive health management plan, identifying and treating common goat ailments, and establishing a strong partnership with a veterinarian, you can ensure the wellbeing and productivity of your goats. The health of your goats directly impacts their growth, reproduction, and overall quality of life. As you prioritize their health needs, you contribute to the sustainability and success of your goat farming venture. By combining preventive measures with timely interventions, you create an environment where your goats can thrive and fulfill their potential as valuable and resilient livestock.

Chapter 6:
Common Goat Diseases and Prevention

In the intricate tapestry of goat farming, the health and wellbeing of your herd are of paramount importance. As a responsible goat steward, it is crucial to be equipped with knowledge about common goat diseases, their symptoms, and effective prevention strategies. This chapter embarks on a journey through the realm of goat health, unraveling the intricacies of various diseases that can affect your caprine companions and providing insights into proactive measures to safeguard their health and vitality.

Understanding Common Goat Diseases

Goats, like any other living beings, are susceptible to a range of diseases and health issues. Familiarizing yourself with these diseases allows you to detect and respond to potential problems early.

Caseous Lymphadenitis (CL): A bacterial infection that leads to abscesses, commonly found in lymph nodes and udders. CL can spread through direct contact or contaminated environments.

Caprine Arthritis Encephalitis (CAE): A viral infection that primarily affects young goats, CAE can lead to arthritis, pneumonia, and encephalitis. The virus is often transmitted through colostrum and milk.

Foot Rot: A contagious bacterial infection affecting hooves, foot rot causes lameness and discomfort. It thrives in damp and unsanitary conditions.

Internal Parasites: Worm infestations, such as gastrointestinal and lung worms, can lead to poor growth, anemia, and even death if left untreated.

External Parasites: Mites, lice, and ticks can cause itching, hair loss, and skin irritation, compromising the wellbeing of your goats.

Identifying Symptoms and Diagnosis

Vigilance in observing your goats' behavior and health is essential for early detection and timely intervention. Recognizing the symptoms of common diseases enables you to take appropriate actions.

Physical Symptoms: Observe changes in appetite, weight loss, coughing, nasal discharge, diarrhea, and abnormal posture. Swellings, abscesses, and changes in behavior may also indicate health issues.

Diagnostic Measures: If you suspect a disease, consult a veterinarian who can perform physical exams, blood tests, fecal exams, and other diagnostic tests to accurately identify the ailment.

Preventive Measures and Management

Preventing common goat diseases involves a combination of management practices, hygiene, and proactive strategies. Implementing these measures helps create a healthier environment for your goats.

Quarantine and Isolation: Isolate new goats before introducing them to the herd to prevent the spread of diseases. Quarantine helps identify any potential health issues before they affect the entire herd.

Vaccination Programs: Consult with a veterinarian to develop a suitable vaccination program based on your location, local disease prevalence, and herd size.

Parasite Management: Implement rotational grazing, proper sanitation, and strategic deworming to control internal and external parasites.

Hygiene and Cleanliness: Maintain clean living areas, provide fresh water, and practice regular hoof trimming to prevent foot-related ailments.

The pursuit of healthy goats encompasses both the art and science of husbandry. By understanding common goat diseases, being vigilant about symptoms, and embracing preventive measures, you assume a role that extends beyond caretaker to guardian of your caprine companions' wellbeing.

As you navigate this chapter, remember that prevention is the cornerstone of goat health. Implementing sound management practices, fostering a hygienic environment, and collaborating with veterinary professionals empower you to mitigate the risks of common diseases and provide your goats with the best chance for a vibrant and thriving life.

In safeguarding the health of your herd, you epitomize the essence of responsible goat farming—a harmonious blend of knowledge, care, and unwavering commitment. Your dedication not only ensures the vitality of your goats but also underscores your role as a protector of the delicate balance between nature and nurture on your farm.

Chapter 7:
Breeding and Reproduction

Bringing New Life to the Farm: Navigating Goat Reproductive Cycles, Selecting Breeding Stock, and Expertly Managing Breeding and Kidding

Breeding goats is a fascinating and essential aspect of goat farming that allows you to expand your herd, improve genetics, and contribute to the sustainability of your farm. This chapter will unravel the intricacies of goat reproductive cycles, guide you through the process of selecting the right breeding stock, and provide you with valuable insights into effectively managing the breeding and kidding process.

Understanding Goat Reproductive Cycles

Goat reproductive cycles are influenced by various factors, including breed, nutrition, and environmental conditions. Generally, goats are considered seasonal breeders, with the onset of breeding season typically coinciding with decreasing daylight hours. This is more pronounced in some breeds, such as Nigerian Dwarf goats, which are known for their strict seasonal breeding patterns. Understanding the estrus cycle—commonly known as heat—is crucial for successful breeding.

Estrus Cycle: The estrus cycle in goats lasts approximately 18 to 21 days. During this time, a doe (female goat) exhibits behavioral changes, such as restlessness, vocalization, and mounting other goats. Paying close attention to these signs helps you identify when a doe is in heat.

Breeding Season: Most goats experience a heightened breeding season in the fall, although some breeds may cycle throughout the year. Proper lighting and nutritional adjustments can influence and extend breeding seasons.

Selecting Breeding Stock

Choosing the right breeding stock is a pivotal decision that directly impacts the quality and productivity of your herd. Breeding stock selection involves evaluating various factors to ensure strong genetics, health, and overall suitability.

Genetic Considerations: Aim to select goats with desirable traits that align with your farm's goals. Whether you're focusing on milk production, meat quality, or fiber yield, a deep understanding of breed standards and genetic inheritance is crucial.

Health and Conformation: Healthy breeding stock is essential for a successful breeding program. Evaluate potential breeding animals for physical conformation, soundness, and absence of hereditary health issues.

Pedigree Analysis: Studying pedigrees helps trace the lineage of potential breeding animals, enabling you to identify any genetic weaknesses or strengths. This information aids in making informed breeding decisions.

Managing Breeding and Kidding

Properly managing the breeding and kidding process ensures the health and wellbeing of both the doe and her offspring. Effective management involves careful planning and meticulous attention to detail.

Breeding Preparation: Before breeding, ensure that does are in optimal health and body condition. Provide a balanced diet, address any health concerns, and administer necessary vaccinations and parasite control measures.

Kidding Preparation: As kidding season approaches, create a comfortable and clean kidding environment. Provide nesting materials, separate expectant does from the herd, and monitor their behavior for signs of impending labor.

Assisting with Kidding: While most goats are capable of kidding without assistance, there are times when intervention is necessary. Be prepared to assist if complications arise, such as mal-positioned kids or prolonged labor.

Newborn Kid Care: Immediately after birth, ensure that newborn kids receive colostrum—a nutrient-rich first milk—within the first few hours. Monitor kids for proper nursing, and provide warmth and shelter during their vulnerable early days.

Breeding and reproduction are pivotal aspects of goat farming that demand knowledge, dedication, and keen observation. By understanding goat reproductive cycles, selecting the right breeding stock, and expertly managing breeding and kidding, you pave the way for a flourishing and sustainable goat herd. The bonds formed with your goats during this rewarding process will undoubtedly deepen your connection to the world of goat farming.

Chapter 8:
Goat Kids Care

Nurturing the Future: A Comprehensive Guide to Preparing for Kidding Season, Providing Proper Care for Newborn Kids, and Ensuring the Growth and Health of Young Goats

Goat kids, those adorable bundles of energy and curiosity, represent the promise of the future on your farm. Caring for these tiny wonders is a rewarding yet intricate task that demands a deep understanding of their unique needs and developmental stages. In this chapter, we will delve into the art and science of goat kids care, covering everything from preparing for kidding season to weaning and fostering healthy growth.

Preparing for Kidding Season

As the days grow shorter and the anticipation mounts, preparing for the upcoming kidding season becomes paramount. This period of excitement and uncertainty requires meticulous planning and thoughtful consideration to ensure the smooth arrival of new kids.

Nesting and Kidding Area: Designate a clean and well-ventilated area for kidding. Provide ample bedding and nesting material to create a cozy and safe space for the does to give birth. Adequate space and privacy reduce stress and promote successful kidding.

Nutritional Readiness: Prior to kidding, ensure that pregnant does receive appropriate nutrition. A balanced diet rich in minerals and vitamins contributes to healthy pregnancies and robust kids.

Kidding Kit: Assemble a well-stocked kidding kit that includes essential supplies such as clean towels, gloves, iodine for umbilical cord care, and a thermometer. Having these items readily available can make a significant difference during the birthing process.

Proper Care of Newborn Kids

Welcoming the arrival of newborn kids is a joyous occasion, but it also marks the beginning of a critical phase in their lives. Adequate care and attention during the first few days are essential for their survival and long-term wellbeing.

Colostrum Feeding: Colostrum, the first milk produced by the doe, is rich in essential nutrients and antibodies that provide vital immunity to the kids. Ensure that each kid receives adequate colostrum within the first few hours of birth to establish a strong foundation for their health.

Umbilical Cord Care: Immediately after birth, disinfect the umbilical cord stump with iodine to prevent infection. Regularly monitor the cord for any signs of swelling or discharge.

Warmth and Shelter: Newborn kids are highly susceptible to cold temperatures. Provide a draft-free shelter and supplemental heat source if necessary, especially during inclement weather. Cold stress can have detrimental effects on their health and growth.

Monitoring and Bonding: Regularly observe the kids to ensure they are nursing and behaving normally. A strong bond with their mother is crucial for their psychological and emotional development.

Weaning and Growing Healthy Kids

As kids grow, the process of weaning them from their mother's milk marks another significant milestone. Proper weaning practices and appropriate growth management contribute to raising robust and healthy young goats.

Weaning Transition: Begin the weaning process gradually, around 8 to 12 weeks of age. Start by introducing solid feeds and reducing milk gradually over a few weeks. This transition minimizes stress and digestive issues.

Balanced Diet: Postweaning, focus on providing a balanced diet that meets the nutritional needs of growing kids. High-quality hay, fresh water, and appropriate grain feeds contribute to steady growth and development.

Exercise and Enrichment: Encourage physical activity and mental stimulation by providing ample space for play and exploration. Proper exercise promotes strong bones and muscles and prevents obesity.

Health Management: Continue regular health checks, vaccinations, and parasite control measures to ensure the wellbeing of growing kids. Address any health concerns promptly to prevent complications.

Raising goat kids is a journey that intertwines joy, responsibility, and the magic of new life. By preparing for kidding season, providing proper care for newborn kids, and guiding their growth through weaning, you play a crucial role in nurturing the future of your herd. Each step you take, from ensuring colostrum intake to creating a safe and enriching environment, contributes to the overall health, vitality, and resilience of your young goats.

The bond formed between you and your kids during these formative stages is one that will endure, and the lessons learned will extend far beyond the boundaries of your farm. As you witness them thrive, grow, and embark on their own journeys, you'll find yourself enriched by the experience and deeply connected to the intricate tapestry of life on the farm. With dedication, knowledge, and a heart full of care, you are well-equipped to shepherd your goat kids towards a future filled with promise and vitality.

Chapter 9:
Milking and Dairy Goat Management

Harvesting Liquid Gold: A Comprehensive Guide to Milking Procedures and Techniques, Proper Handling and Storage of Milk, and the Art of Processing and Utilizing Dairy Products from Your Dairy Goats

Dairy goats are the heartbeats of a homestead, providing a continuous stream of nourishing milk that forms the foundation of various culinary delights. Milking these gentle and productive animals is a skill that marries tradition with science, yielding not only creamy goodness but also a sense of fulfillment and connection to the land. In this chapter, we embark on a journey through the world of milking and dairy goat management, delving into the intricacies of milking techniques, the art of milk handling, and the transformation of milk into delectable dairy products.

Milking Procedures and Techniques

The act of milking is an art that requires patience, precision, and a deep understanding of goat behavior. Establishing a routine and employing proper techniques ensure a stress-free and productive milking experience.

Sanitary Practices: Before milking, thoroughly clean the udder and teats to prevent contamination. Wash your hands, wear clean milking attire, and sanitize equipment to maintain milk quality and prevent bacterial growth.

Milking Routine: Create a consistent milking routine that aligns with your goat's natural schedule. Milking at the same times each day helps maintain udder health and milk production.

Milking Equipment: Invest in high-quality milking equipment, such as a sanitized milking bucket, teat cups, and a milking machine if preferred. Properly fitted teat cups ensure gentle and efficient milking.

Hand Milking: If hand milking, master the art of hand placement, rhythm, and pressure. Gently squeeze and release each teat to mimic the natural nursing action of kids, ensuring complete milk extraction.

Handling and Storing Milk

Once the precious milk is harvested, proper handling and storage are paramount to preserving its freshness and nutritional value. Following hygienic practices and maintaining optimal temperature conditions safeguard the quality of your milk.

Immediate Cooling: Rapidly cool the milk to around 40°F (4°C) or lower to inhibit bacterial growth. Use a cooling tank or cold water bath to quickly lower the milk's temperature.

Filtering: Strain the milk through a fine mesh filter to remove any impurities or debris. Clean filters between uses to prevent cross-contamination.

Storage Containers: Store milk in food-grade, sanitized containers specifically designed for milk storage. Glass or food-grade plastic containers with airtight lids are ideal.

Refrigeration or Freezing: For short-term storage, refrigerate milk at temperatures below 40°F (4°C). For longer storage, freeze milk in small, labeled portions, leaving room for expansion.

Processing and Utilizing Dairy Products

From creamy butter to artisan cheeses, the possibilities for transforming goat milk into delectable dairy products are virtually endless. Mastering the art of processing allows you to savor a diverse range of homemade dairy delights.

Pasteurization: If desired, pasteurize raw milk by heating it to a specific temperature for a set duration to eliminate harmful pathogens while retaining flavor and nutritional quality.

Homemade Butter: Churn fresh cream to create rich and flavorful homemade butter. Experiment with salted and unsalted variations, and infuse with herbs or spices for unique flavors.

Cheese Making: Embark on the captivating journey of cheese making. From soft, tangy chèvre to aged, robust cheddar, cheese making offers a chance to explore your culinary creativity.

Yogurt and Kefir: Cultivate beneficial probiotics by crafting your own yogurt or kefir. These cultured dairy products not only taste delightful but also offer health-enhancing properties.

Ice Cream and Custards: Transform your milk into luscious ice creams, custards, and puddings that capture the essence of freshness and indulgence.

Milking and dairy goat management are a harmonious blend of science, tradition, and craftsmanship. As you master the art of milking procedures and techniques, elevate your milk handling and storage practices, and venture into the realm of dairy product processing, you embark on a journey that epitomizes self-sufficiency and a profound connection to your farm's resources.

The act of milking, once performed with care and dedication, yields not only sustenance but also a sense of accomplishment. The process of handling and storing milk with meticulous precision safeguards the fruits of your labor, while the transformative journey of creating dairy products unfolds the endless possibilities locked within each drop of milk.

As you savor the fruits of your labor, from a spoonful of creamy yogurt to a slice of freshly baked cheese-laden bread, remember that you are not just a farmer but also an artisan—a steward of nature's bounty. The knowledge and skills gained in milking and dairy goat management empower you to create and savor the taste of a truly wholesome and homemade life.

Chapter 10:
Fiber Goats and Their Care

From Fleece to Finery: Unraveling the World of Angora and Cashmere Goat Breeds, Mastering Shearing and Fiber Processing, and Creating an Array of Exquisite Products from Goat Fiber

Amidst the pastoral landscape of goat farming, two exceptional breeds stand out for their luxurious contributions to the world of textiles—the Angora and Cashmere goats. These remarkable animals offer a renewable resource that weaves a tale of opulence, craftsmanship, and sustainability. In this chapter, we embark on a journey through the realm of fiber goats and their care, exploring the unique characteristics of Angora and Cashmere breeds, mastering the art of shearing and fiber processing, and discovering the diverse range of products that can be crafted from their exquisite fiber.

Angora and Cashmere Goat Breeds

Angora and Cashmere goats are revered for their exquisite fleece, each with its own distinct qualities that make them prized assets for fiber enthusiasts and artisans.

Angora Goats: With their lustrous and silky Mohair fiber, Angora goats captivate the senses. Native to Turkey, these goats produce an array of luxurious and versatile fibers that range from fine and delicate to robust and strong.

Cashmere Goats: Hailing from the rugged terrains of Central Asia, Cashmere goats bestow upon us the coveted Cashmere fiber. This downy, fine fiber is renowned for its unparalleled softness and warmth, making it a treasure for crafting luxurious garments.

Shearing and Processing Fiber

The process of shearing and processing goat fiber is an art that requires precision and care. Skillfully handling these steps ensures that the harvested fleece retains its quality and potential.

Shearing Technique: Employ gentle and careful shearing techniques to harvest the fleece without causing stress or discomfort to the goat. Proper restraint and skilled hands are essential to a successful shearing process.

Fiber Sorting: After shearing, sort the fleece based on fiber length, color, and texture. This preliminary step lays the foundation for creating consistent and high-quality fiber products.

Cleaning and Washing: Thoroughly clean and wash the raw fiber to remove dirt, grease, and contaminants. Gentle detergents and warm water help preserve the fiber's natural luster and texture.

Utilizing Goat Fiber for Various Products

The journey from raw fiber to finished product is a transformative one, yielding an array of textiles that showcase the beauty and versatility of Angora and Cashmere goat fibers.

Spinning and Yarn: Transform cleaned and carded fiber into luscious yarn through the art of spinning. Various spinning techniques result in yarns of different textures, thicknesses, and color blends.

Weaving and Knitting: Yarn spun from Angora and Cashmere fibers can be woven or knitted into an assortment of textiles, from delicate shawls to cozy sweaters and blankets.

Felting and Fiber Art: Embrace the world of felting to create intricate fiber art pieces, accessories, and sculptures. The unique qualities of Angora and Cashmere fibers contribute to the texture and character of the final creations.

Dyeing and Embellishing: Experiment with natural or synthetic dyes to add vibrant hues to your fiber creations. Embellish your textiles with embroidery, beading, or other decorative techniques.

Fiber goats, with their sumptuous fleece, offer a world of creative possibilities that bridge the realms of agriculture and artistry. The process of tending to Angora and Cashmere goats, shearing their fleece, and transforming it into exquisite products is a harmonious symphony of nature's offerings and human ingenuity.

As you immerse yourself in the care of these remarkable animals and explore the art of fiber processing, you become a custodian of a time-honored tradition—one that connects you to the artisans of the past and the creative potential of the future. With each skein of yarn spun, every loom thread woven, and every delicate garment created, you're not only crafting textiles but also weaving the threads of history and imagination.

The journey of fiber goats and their care invites you to be both steward and artist, blending the elegance of nature's fibers with the vision of your creative spirit. As you craft textiles that showcase the magnificence of Angora and Cashmere fibers, you embark on a voyage that is as enriching and captivating as the fibers themselves.

Chapter 11:
Meat Production and Butchering

From Pasture to Plate: A Comprehensive Exploration of Raising Boer and Kiko Meat Goats, Strategic Growth and Nutritional Management, and Compassionate and Skillful Butchering Practices

The world of goat farming encompasses not only the realm of companionship and fiber, but also the bountiful realm of meat production. Among the diverse goat breeds, Boer and Kiko goats stand tall as champions of meat production, offering succulent and flavorful meat that graces tables around the world. In this chapter, we embark on a journey through the intricacies of meat production and butchering, unveiling the art of raising Boer and Kiko meat goats, unraveling strategies for growth and nutrition, and delving into the realm of humane and efficient butchering practices.

Raising Meat Goats: Boers and Kikos

Boer and Kiko goats are two breeds that have gained widespread recognition for their exceptional meat quality and adaptability to various environments.

Boer Goats: Originating from South Africa, Boer goats are renowned for their fast growth, muscular build, and high meat-to-bone ratio. Their distinctive appearance and ability to thrive on diverse forage make them sought-after meat producers.

Kiko Goats: Hailing from New Zealand, Kiko goats boast remarkable resilience and adaptability. Their robust nature, resistance to parasites, and efficient foraging abilities contribute to their reputation as a prized meat breed.

Managing Growth and Nutrition for Meat Production
Efficiently managing the growth and nutrition of meat goats is a cornerstone of successful meat production. Strategic feeding and care contribute to the development of healthy, well-muscled animals ready for the butchering process.

Balanced Nutrition: Provide a well-balanced diet rich in protein, energy, vitamins, and minerals. Tailor feeding programs to match the specific growth stages and nutritional needs of meat goats.

Pasture Management: Utilize rotational grazing systems to ensure goats have access to fresh, high-quality forage. Proper pasture management not only supports optimal growth but also aids in parasite control.

Supplemental Feeding: Depending on the availability of forage, offer supplemental feeds such as grain, hay, and mineral supplements. Consistency and quality in feeding contribute to steady growth rates.

Humane and Efficient Butchering Practices
The culmination of the meat production journey lies in the art of butchering—an endeavor that demands both skill and compassion. Implementing humane and efficient practices ensures that the meat is harvested with respect for the animal's life and quality of the final product.

Slaughter Techniques: Choose slaughter methods that prioritize minimal stress and discomfort for the animal. Swift and humane methods, such as captive bolt stunning or electrical stunning, help ensure a stress-free process.

Processing Procedures: Efficiently process the carcass to yield high-quality meat cuts. Knowledge of anatomy and proper knife skills are essential to achieve clean and precise cuts.

Meat Handling and Storage: After butchering, handle and store meat in a manner that maintains freshness and safety. Proper chilling or freezing prevents spoilage and preserves meat quality.

Utilizing All Parts: Embrace the ethos of nose-to-tail eating by utilizing all parts of the animal. This approach not only maximizes meat utilization but also honors the animal's sacrifice.

The journey of meat production and butchering is a multifaceted exploration that intertwines husbandry, nutrition, and craftsmanship. As you raise Boer and Kiko meat goats, master the art of strategic growth and nutrition, and embrace humane and efficient butchering practices, you engage in a process that respects the cycle of life and nourishes the bodies and souls of those who partake in the harvest.

The meat produced from your efforts is more than just sustenance; it is a culmination of dedication, care, and a deep connection to the land and its creatures. By committing to raising and butchering meat goats with expertise and compassion, you contribute to the rich tapestry of food culture and become a steward of responsible and ethical meat production.

From the pastures where goats graze to the plates where meals are savored, your role in the journey of meat production and butchering brings a profound sense of fulfillment and a renewed appreciation for the delicate balance between life and sustenance. As you continue on this journey, may you find satisfaction in knowing that your efforts contribute to the nourishment of both body and soul.

Chapter 12:
Sustainable and Organic Goat Farming

Nurturing Nature: A Holistic Guide to Embracing Sustainable Practices, Exploring Organic Feeding and Medication Alternatives, and Navigating Certification and Marketing of Organic Goat Products

In the heart of modern agriculture, a movement is flourishing—one that reverberates with the ethos of sustainability and the rhythm of nature. Sustainable and organic goat farming has emerged as a beacon of responsible stewardship, emphasizing harmony with the environment, animal wellbeing, and the production of pure and wholesome products. This chapter embarks on a journey through the realm of sustainable and organic goat farming, unveiling the art of implementing ecologically sound practices, exploring alternatives in organic feeding and medication, and navigating the path to certification and effective marketing of organic goat products.

Implementing Sustainable Practices

Sustainable goat farming is a commitment to nurturing the land, conserving resources, and fostering a balance between production and preservation. By implementing a range of eco-conscious practices, you become a guardian of both your herd and the environment.

Rotational Grazing: Divide pasture areas into sections and rotate goats to different sections periodically. This prevents overgrazing, supports soil health, and minimizes parasite loads.

Natural Fertilization: Harness the power of goat manure as a natural fertilizer for your fields. Proper composting and application contribute to soil fertility and plant growth.

Agroforestry: Integrate trees and shrubs into your farm layout. These not only provide shade and shelter for goats but also aid in erosion control and biodiversity conservation.

Water Management: Employ efficient water management techniques such as rainwater harvesting and proper irrigation to minimize wastage and ensure water availability for both goats and crops.

Organic Feeding and Medication Options

Organic goat farming places a premium on natural inputs, avoiding synthetic chemicals and promoting the health of animals and consumers alike. Thoughtful choices in feeding and medication support the wellbeing of your goats while adhering to organic principles.

Organic Feed: Source organic feeds and forages that are free from genetically modified organisms (GMOs) and synthetic additives. Opt for whole grains, legumes, and locally sourced feeds whenever possible.

Herbal and Natural Remedies: Explore herbal supplements and natural remedies for managing common goat health issues. Herbal treatments, essential oils, and homeopathic remedies can contribute to the wellbeing of your herd.

Parasite Control: Employ rotational grazing, strategic pasture management, and targeted deworming schedules to minimize parasite loads naturally.

Certification and Marketing of Organic Goat Products
Certifying your goat farm as organic not only validates your commitment to sustainable practices but also opens doors to a niche market that values pure and ethically produced products. Navigating certification and effective marketing strategies are integral to reaping the rewards of your organic efforts.

Certification Process: Research and choose a recognized organic certification agency. Prepare your farm to meet their standards, which may include maintaining detailed records and undergoing inspections.

Labeling and Packaging: Design labels that clearly communicate your organic certification and sustainable practices. Utilize ecofriendly packaging to further align with your commitment to the environment.

Market Research: Understand your target audience and identify potential markets for your organic goat products. Collaborate with local farmers' markets, coops, and specialty stores to showcase your offerings.

Educational Outreach: Engage in educational initiatives to raise awareness about the benefits of organic goat products. Connect with consumers through workshops, social media, and farm tours to foster a loyal customer base.

Sustainable and organic goat farming is more than a practice—it's a philosophy that harmonizes with the rhythms of nature and cultivates a legacy of responsible stewardship. By embracing ecologically sound practices, exploring organic feeding and medication alternatives, and navigating the realms of certification and marketing, you embark on a journey that reverberates with purpose and integrity.

Your commitment to sustainability and organic principles extends beyond the boundaries of your farm; it resonates with a growing movement that prioritizes the wellbeing of animals, land, and consumers. As you navigate this chapter, may your efforts serve as a beacon of inspiration for fellow farmers, consumers, and future generations. By nurturing nature, you become a guardian of the delicate tapestry of life, weaving together the threads of responsible farming, environmental consciousness, and the wholesome nourishment of organic goat products.

Chapter 13:
Business and Marketing Considerations

Nurturing Prosperity: A Comprehensive Guide to Crafting a Business Plan for Goat Farming, Mastering the Art of Marketing Your Goat Products, and Forging Strong Connections with Local Markets and Customers

In the dynamic realm of goat farming, success is not only measured by the health and happiness of your herd but also by the viability and reach of your business. Crafting a thriving goat farming venture requires a keen understanding of business principles, effective marketing strategies, and the art of connecting with local markets and customers. This chapter embarks on a journey through the intricacies of business and marketing considerations, unraveling the process of developing a comprehensive business plan, illuminating the path to effectively market your goat products, and guiding you in fostering strong and lasting relationships with local markets and customers.

Developing a Business Plan for Goat Farming

A well-structured business plan serves as the compass that guides your goat farming journey. It outlines your goals, strategies, and financial projections, providing a roadmap for success.

Defining Objectives: Clearly articulate your short-term and long-term goals for your goat farming venture. Are you focused on meat, milk, fiber, or a combination? Determine your production and sales targets.

Market Research: Conduct thorough research to understand the demand for your goat products, pricing trends, and potential competitors. Identify your target market and assess consumer preferences.

Financial Projections: Create detailed financial projections that encompass startup costs, ongoing expenses, revenue forecasts, and profit margins. Develop a realistic budget that accounts for all aspects of your operation.

Operations Plan: Outline the daily operations of your goat farm, including feeding routines, health management practices, breeding strategies, and herd maintenance.

Marketing Your Goat Products

Effective marketing is the bridge that connects your farm to consumers, conveying the unique value of your goat products and forging lasting relationships.

Branding and Identity: Develop a compelling brand identity that reflects your farm's values, mission, and unique offerings. A well-crafted brand establishes a strong foundation for your marketing efforts.

Product Packaging: Design visually appealing and informative packaging for your goat products. Labels should communicate key details such as product type, origin, and any special attributes (e.g., organic, pasture raised).

Online Presence: Create a professional and user-friendly website that showcases your products, farm story, and contact information. Utilize social media platforms to engage with your audience and share farm updates.

Farm Events and Workshops: Host farm tours, workshops, and events that offer consumers an opportunity to connect with your goats, learn about your farming practices, and gain firsthand experience.

Connecting with Local Markets and Customers

Building strong relationships with local markets and customers is a cornerstone of successful goat farming. These connections not only bolster sales but also create a sense of community and loyalty.

Farmers' Markets: Participate in local farmers' markets to showcase your goat products and interact directly with consumers. Farmers' markets provide a platform for building relationships and receiving immediate feedback.

Collaborations and Partnerships: Collaborate with local restaurants, chefs, and artisanal food producers to feature your goat products in their offerings. Partnerships expand your market reach and enhance your product's visibility.

Community Engagement: Engage with your local community through outreach initiatives, workshops, and educational events. Position yourself as a valuable resource and advocate for sustainable and ethical farming.

Customer Feedback: Actively seek and respond to customer feedback. Consider implementing loyalty programs, surveys, and promotions to strengthen customer relationships and gain insights for improvement.

The tapestry of goat farming extends far beyond the pastures and barns—it weaves a narrative of business acumen, marketing finesse, and meaningful connections with consumers. By developing a comprehensive business plan, mastering the art of marketing, and forging strong bonds with local markets and customers, you embark on a journey that transforms your passion into a thriving and sustainable venture.

In the landscape of business and marketing considerations, you emerge as a visionary, a communicator, and a steward of quality and integrity. The efforts you invest in branding, outreach, and customer engagement not only elevate your goat products but also contribute to the fabric of your local community.

As you navigate this chapter, may your farm's story resonate with authenticity and purpose, capturing the hearts and palates of those who partake in the bounty of your labor. By nurturing prosperity through thoughtful planning, effective marketing, and genuine connections, you become not only a goat farmer but also a custodian of a legacy that enriches lives and celebrates the essence of responsible and rewarding goat farming.

Chapter 14:
Troubleshooting and Problem Solving

Navigating the Goat Farmer's Compass: A Comprehensive Guide to Addressing Common Challenges, Unraveling Solutions to Goat Related Issues, and Knowing When to Seek Professional Help

In the intricate tapestry of goat farming, challenges and unexpected situations are as much a part of the journey as the joys and triumphs. A seasoned goat farmer possesses the ability to troubleshoot and problem solve with grace and confidence, adapting to the everchanging landscape of goat care. This chapter embarks on a journey through the realm of troubleshooting and problem solving, equipping you with the knowledge to address common challenges, offering insights into finding solutions to goat related issues, and guiding you in recognizing when it's time to seek professional assistance.

Dealing with Common Challenges

Goat farming presents an array of challenges that require careful consideration and proactive management. Understanding these challenges empowers you to respond effectively and minimize their impact.

Parasite Infestations: Goats are prone to internal and external parasites. Implement rotational grazing, maintain clean living conditions, and develop a deworming schedule to manage parasite loads.

Nutritional Imbalances: Poor nutrition can lead to various health issues. Consult with a veterinarian or nutritionist to ensure your goats receive a balanced diet that meets their specific needs.

Reproductive Challenges: Breeding, kidding, and fertility issues can arise. Proper management of breeding schedules, nutritional support, and prenatal care can mitigate reproductive challenges.

Hoof Health: Neglected hooves can lead to discomfort and lameness. Regular hoof trimming and proper sanitation prevent hoof issues and promote overall wellbeing.

Finding Solutions to Goat Related Issues

Effective problem solving is a skill that emerges from observation, research, and adaptability. By delving into the intricacies of goat behavior and health, you can unearth solutions to a wide range of goat related issues.

Research and Education: Utilize reputable resources, such as veterinary manuals, agricultural universities, and online forums, to gather information on specific issues affecting your goats.

Observation and Diagnosis: Observe your goats closely to identify changes in behavior, appetite, and overall health. Early detection allows you to address issues before they escalate.

Consulting Experts: Reach out to veterinarians, experienced goat farmers, and animal health professionals for guidance. Their expertise can provide valuable insights and solutions.

When to Seek Professional Help

Recognizing the limits of your knowledge and seeking professional assistance when necessary is a hallmark of responsible goat farming. Certain situations warrant the expertise of veterinarians or other specialized professionals.

Medical Emergencies: In cases of severe injury, illness, or birthing complications, immediate veterinary attention is essential. Delay can exacerbate the situation.

Diagnostic Challenges: If you're unable to identify the cause of a goat's ailment or issue, consult a veterinarian who can conduct diagnostic tests and provide accurate diagnoses.

Specialized Treatments: Conditions requiring specialized treatments, surgeries, or advanced medical procedures should be entrusted to professionals with the necessary training and equipment.

The journey of goat farming is a testament to your dedication, resilience, and willingness to embrace both triumphs and challenges. As you navigate the realm of troubleshooting and problem solving, you step into the role of a detective, investigator, and advocate for your goats' wellbeing.

By addressing common challenges, seeking out solutions to goat related issues, and knowing when to call in professional help, you not only safeguard the health and happiness of your herd but also deepen your understanding of goat husbandry. This chapter equips you with the tools to meet challenges head-on, respond with confidence, and ensure that the journey of goat farming remains one of growth, learning, and the unwavering commitment to the care and wellbeing of your caprine companions.

Conclusion

As we draw the final threads of this comprehensive guide on goat farming, we find ourselves immersed in a tapestry woven with knowledge, passion, and dedication. The journey of goat farming is one that transcends the ordinary, embracing the intricate dance between human stewardship and the natural world. From the gentle bleating of newborn kids to the rich harvest of milk, fiber, and meat, every aspect of goat farming reflects the harmony of tradition, innovation, and the enduring bond between farmer and animal.

Throughout these chapters, we have delved into the diverse realms of goat husbandry, each thread contributing to the vibrant fabric of your journey. From the foundational principles of goat care and management to the intricacies of breeding, milking, and fiber processing, you have embarked on a voyage that celebrates the artistry of nurturing life and reaping its rewards.

In nurturing your caprine companions, you have embraced the roles of caretaker, healer, and advocate. You have learned to decipher the language of gestures, to understand the rhythm of behavior, and to respond to the calls of nature's rhythms. With each step, you have fostered an understanding of sustainable and organic practices, ensuring that your farm not only flourishes but also stands as a testament to ethical and responsible farming.

As you chart your course through the chapters on business, marketing, and troubleshooting, you stand at the intersection of stewardship and entrepreneurship. You have honed the skills to not only care for your herd but also to share the fruits of your labor with a community that values the purity and integrity of your offerings. Your farm becomes a beacon, radiating the spirit of collaboration, innovation, and conscious consumerism.

In concluding this journey, we celebrate your role as a custodian of tradition and a pioneer of progress. Your commitment to goat farming echoes through time, connecting you to generations of farmers who have tilled the land, tended to animals, and woven the fabric of sustenance and livelihood. As you tread this path, may the knowledge shared within these pages continue to guide your endeavors, infusing them with wisdom, compassion, and the joy of a life well lived.

In the rustic symphony of goat farms, may your farm be a harmonious chord that resonates with the echoes of history and the promise of a future nurtured by the love and dedication you pour into every aspect of your craft. As you continue to tend to your herd, may your journey be marked by fulfillment, growth, and the enduring connection between you, your goats, and the timeless dance of the land.